Pruning
Ornamental Shrubs

A Wisley Handbook

Pruning
Ornamental Shrubs

JOHN CLAYTON revised by JOHN MAIN

Cassell

The Royal Horticultural Society

THE ROYAL HORTICULTURAL SOCIETY

Cassell Educational Limited
Villiers House, 41/47 Strand
London WC2N 5JE
for the Royal Horticultural Society

First published 1973
Second edition 1986
Third edition 1992

British Library Cataloguing in Publication Data
A catalogue record for this book is available from the
British Library

ISBN 0-304-32023-4

Photographs by Photos Horticultural

Phototypesetting by Chapterhouse Ltd, Formby
Printed in Hong Kong by Wing King Tong Co. Ltd

Cover: pruning *Cornus alba* at Wisley.
  Photograph by Wilf Halliday/RHS
p. 1: *Pyracantha* and *Parthenocissus tricuspidata* as autumn approaches.
p. 2: *Ceanothus impressus* 'Puget Blue'.
Back cover: *Wisteria sinensis*.
  Photographs by Photos Horticultural

Contents

Introduction

Pruning is an important garden operation and one which can materially improve the beauty, health and vigour of many of our ornamental shrubs. Although it may seem somewhat complicated at first, once the basic principles and methods have been understood it becomes an interesting and rewarding process. It is the object of this handbook to explain and illustrate these operations, so that the amateur gardener may be encouraged to get the best display from his shrubs.

Opposite above: *Cornus alba* 'Sibirica', one of the dogwoods, which may be pruned annually for bark effect (see p. 17).
Opposite below: *Buddleja alternifolia* (left) should be pruned immediately after flowering, while *B. davidii* (right) should be pruned when growth begins in early spring (see p. 48).
Below: *Ribes sanguineum*, the flowering currant, which should be pruned immediately after flowering in spring (see p. 60).

What do we mean by pruning? The dictionary definition is: 'The removal of any part of a tree or shrub, either stem, branches or roots, in order to direct the energies of growth into channels desired by the cultivator'. In other words, we are cutting away part of a plant to achieve a particular effect, and it is the decision as to which parts to remove, and when, that often presents some problems to the amateur gardener.

Before dealing with the operations in more detail it should be understood that not all shrubs need to be pruned every year. Many can be left to grow to mature specimens with no more attention than occasionally removing a piece of dead or damaged wood, or a branch which has grown awkwardly and is spoiling the shape and balance of the plant.

But if we are going to grow shrubs in our gardens, there is one important thing to remember – unless we are very careful to choose the right plant for a particular position, we may well find that we have increased the need for pruning instead of reducing it. All shrubs will grow until they have reached their natural size, and if we have selected a species or variety of, say, a forsythia or flowering currant which normally grows to 6 or 8 feet tall (1.8 to 2.4 m), this may later require drastic cutting back to keep it within the limits of the space allotted to it. By taking the trouble to study catalogues and seek advice from a nurseryman or someone familiar with local conditions, it is usually possible to find the right shrub for even the most unpromising position.

However, many of our most useful shrubs do respond to regular annual pruning, and we can now go on to consider the three main reasons for this operation.

The Moroccan broom, *Cytisus battanderi*, should have old growths thinned out after flowering (see p. 52).

The objects of pruning

To keep the shrub in good health.
To maintain the shape and balance of the shrub.
To produce from it the best decorative effect.

KEEPING THE SHRUB HEALTHY

This is a very important aspect of pruning. Many serious diseases of plants spread most easily to shrubs which are in poor health and particularly those with dead or damaged branches. These may extend into healthy tissues even killing the plant. Broken branches and those which rub together in the wind, causing the protective covering of the bark to be bruised or broken, are also potential sources of infection.

Good cultivation is one way in which we can help to increase the natural resistance of a shrub to disease. Enrichment of the soil before planting, followed by feeding, watering and the application of a soil mulch, are all ways in which we can encourage the shrub to produce vigorous, healthy growth. Damage may still occur, however, and the longer damaged wood is allowed to remain on the plant, the greater the risk of disease. It is essential that all dead, broken or bruised branches are cut cleanly back into healthy living tissue, as soon as damage is noticed. Such prunings should be collected and burned on the bonfire or incinerator.

When we look carefully at a shrub, we can see that the best flowers and healthiest leaves are borne on the top and outside of the plant. In the middle of the bush, where they may be starved of light and air, the growths tend to be weak and thin. Not only do the healthy vigorous branches produce the best flowers but, because the sun and air can get at them to harden the bark and wood (called ripening) they are more resistant to severe cold than are immature, weak growths. Clearly, then, when we are pruning we must try to keep the centre of the plant fairly open, cutting out completely all thin, weak or crossing shoots, and allowing only the healthiest and most vigorous to remain.

It is also desirable to encourage the production of a regular supply of young, vigorous growths from the base, or at least from low down in the shrub. This will prevent it from becoming top heavy, and also provide replacements for any of the older branches which may be damaged or which become exhausted, and have to be removed.

Above: *Actinidia kolomikta* needs regular winter pruning to keep it under control (see p. 47). Below: all types of *Philadelphus* are pruned immediately after flowering (see p. 59).

Above: *Jasminum nudiflorum* should be cut back to about two pairs of buds as soon as the blooms fade (see p. 56). Below: *Celastrus orbiculatus* needs no pruning if allowed to clamber up a tree (see p. 50).

MAINTAINING SHAPE AND BALANCE

Many of the shrubs in our gardens are grown as single specimens to be viewed from different angles, and even when they form part of a group in a border, they need to be well shaped and evenly balanced. This is normally achieved by pruning, and in its simplest forms entails cutting away any branch which may develop and grow out awkwardly, spoiling the natural form and symmetry of the shrub.

When pruning to maintain shape, it is important to appreciate that there will be a long-term as well as an immediate reaction to a pruning cut, and that by pruning in the wrong way, the result may well be the exact opposite of what was intended. Development of a shrub occurs through the growth buds placed along the branches, sometimes alternately, sometimes opposite one another, sometimes in clusters. This development growth is sustained by food passing up the stem from the root system, and the amount which reaches the bud clearly depends on the diameter of the stem. Obviously more will be able to travel along a plump healthy branch than through a thin weak one.

In annual pruning, all cuts are made in relation to one of the growth buds, and we speak of 'severe' or 'light' pruning according to the proportion of the stem removed. A greater or lesser number of buds are removed according to the degree of severity of the cut, and the number remaining varies accordingly. The amount of food passing up the stem is the same, but in the case of severe pruning this is shared amongst perhaps only two or three buds, whereas in light pruning the number may be six or eight, or even more. Clearly we may expect to get much stronger growth from the former than the latter, and we therefore establish the important principle, that severe pruning promotes a vigorous growth reaction and *vice versa*.

If we now apply this principle to our efforts to maintain shape and balance in a shrub, we can understand why it is so important to look ahead and try to envisage the reaction of the plant to any cuts that we make. Often we find a shrub growing unevenly, with strong healthy branches on one side, and only weak, twiggy growth on the other; our natural impulse may be to cut the strong growth hard back in order to bring it down to the same height as the other side of the plant. But this would, in fact, only achieve exactly the opposite effect, since the vigorous reaction of the severely pruned healthy branches would result in the production of strong growth on the same side of the plant, thus accentuating its unbalanced state.

The answer is to prune the weak growth severely, in the hope of obtaining one or two vigorous branches which will balance up with the lightly pruned stems on the opposite side, where the resultant growth has been comparatively short.

In carrying out such pruning of this type, it may well take more than one season to bring a badly neglected shrub back into proper shape and balance. But as long as we understand the principles behind what we are doing, then we shall achieve the desired effect in the end.

NEWLY PLANTED SHRUBS

With many shrubs, the pruning that is carried out during the first year or two after planting will be somewhat different from that which they need once they have become established.

We expect the nurseryman to supply us with a bushy, well-shaped shrub, with a good, well-developed root system which is more important than the top growth in helping the plant to become properly established.

Even so, not much new growth may be made during the first season, especially if the weather is adverse. But once the root system has become established we may expect to get strong branches developing, and it is in the first two or three years that our pruning will need to be fairly severe, in order to encourage the production of vigorous growth from the base of the plant, which will build up a good shapely framework, on which the shrub can develop in later years.

REJUVENATION OF OVERGROWN SHRUBS

Many shrubs, particularly lilacs, the stronger-growing *Philadelphus*, and viburnums, are capable of developing into really large specimens, perhaps 12 to 15 feet (3.6 to 4.5 m) or more in height. When this stage is reached they may not only be occupying far too much space, but with maturity much of their initial vigour and beauty may have been lost. Any flowers are likely to be borne on the top of the plant, well above eye-level, where their colour will be lost against the sky, and there may well be a lot of dead wood or weak, thin growth in the centre of the plant.

Overgrown shrubs of this type can often be rejuvenated by drastic pruning. But, before deciding to carry this out, one should consider carefully whether the plant may not be too old, when there is little chance of success. It may be better to remove the shrub altogether, and replace it with a young, vigorous specimen.

If it is decided that drastic pruning might be effective, the

13

Above: *Campsis grandiflora* should be pruned in February or early March (see p. 49).
Below: *Caesalpinia japonica* is cut hard back in February (see p. 49).

Above: the Japanese quinces are excellent trained against a wall (see p. 50).
Below: *Eucalyptus* can be restrained by cutting the stems right back (see p. 53).

operation can be done during the dormant season, when there is possibly more time available to tackle the heavier work involved, or for deciduous shrubs such as lilacs or viburnums immediately after flowering. Evergreens such as rhododendrons and conifers of all types should only be dealt with in late spring, May or early June, when they will respond best to such severe treatment.

Any thin weak stems originating low down in the shrub are removed completely and the main stems are then cut hard back to some 2 or 3 feet from ground level (60–90 cm). These may well be 4 to 6 inches in diameter (10 to 15 cm), and it will be necessary to use a good pruning saw, trimming the cuts cleanly with a sharp knife. On such large stems it will probably be difficult to see the positions of the dormant buds, but in fact there will be plenty of them present, and one need not be too particular in selecting the place at which to make the cut. It is usually best to deal with the whole plant at once, provided that it is in good health, and likely to respond quickly to this severe pruning. Alternatively, only a proportion of the stems can be reduced, leaving the remainder to provide some flower until their turn comes a year later.

During the first growing season after such drastic treatment, a large number of growths will develop from the dormant buds on the stems, and if all of them are allowed to remain, they will quickly smother each other. During the next winter most are therefore cut cleanly back to the main stem with a sharp knife, leaving only two or three of the strongest which are allowed to grow on to provide the framework of the rejuvenated bush. In the second and possibly even in the third year, further sucker growth may appear, but it will soon diminish and should be cut out in the same way.

Such treatment is quite a shock to a plant and everything possible should be done to help the shrub to get over the drastic reduction in size and to encourage it to make fresh growth. Generous feeding, in late spring, using a slow release fertilizer such as Enmag, and ample watering during dry weather, as well as a mulch of well-rotted manure or garden compost over the rooting area will help prevent excessive loss of moisture.

ROOT PRUNING

This is an operation which is more commonly carried out on fruit trees, but it has some application to ornamental shrubs, especially in order to check excessive top growth, to restrict the speed of root growth and to prevent them from impoverishing the soil in which other plants are growing. It is also widely used in preparing a large shrub, particularly an evergreen or a conifer which has not recently been transplanted, for its move to a new position.

A trench about 18 inches deep (45 cm) and 12 to 18 inches wide (30 to 45 cm) is dug out around the perimeter of the spread of the branches, and this should expose some of the finer feeding roots, as well as a proportion of the thick anchoring roots. If no roots are found it will be necessary to carefully fork back into the root ball until roots are found. The latter should be cut through on either side of the trench and the central piece of the root removed, care being taken to avoid damaging the feeding roots; the trench should then be refilled. If the shrub is growing in an exposed position it may be necessary to secure it against wind damage after such treatment, either by tying it to a stout stake or, if it is too large for this, securing it by attaching guy wires to posts driven into the ground on three sides of the plant.

When preparing a shrub for transplanting, after exposing and cutting the roots, the trench is refilled with a mixture of soil, garden compost or leafmould and fertilizer, which will encourage the production of fine feeding roots and help the shrub to establish itself quickly in its new position. This operation should be carried out sufficiently far ahead of transplanting to allow time for the new feeding roots to develop; for broad-leaved evergreens and conifers it is best done in the late spring (April or May), when new growth is just beginning, before moving in early autumn, when weather conditions are likely to be most suitable.

OBTAINING THE MAXIMUM DECORATIVE EFFECT

Although we tend to think mainly of ornamental shrubs as having beautiful flowers, there are several other characters which can be of equal decorative value, and which may well have a considerably longer period of effect than two or three weeks of flower. These characters include leaf shape and colour (of particular importance in variegated forms), beauty of fruit, stem colour, the characteristic shape and outline of the shrub, and its screening value or the protection that it affords to other plants.

All of these can be considerably enhanced by correct pruning, in ways which will be considered in detail later. One example which may be mentioned here is the annual hard pruning of forms of dogwood (Cornus) in late March to encourage the production of long, unbranched, one-year-old stems, which have more brightly coloured bark for winter effect than the short twiggy growths on the older wood.

Pruning tools

Pruning does not require an elaborate set of tools; the gardener will be able to manage quite satisfactorily with a good knife and a pair of secateurs. It is only when old overgrown specimens have to be dealt with or some hard dead wood requires cutting out, that a stronger tool, such as a small saw or a pair of short-handled shrub pruners will be needed.

Quality pays, with cutting tools as with anything else, and the extra cost of a really well-balanced and efficient pair of secateurs, or a pruning knife of the correct shape with a blade of the best quality steel, will be repaid many times over by the ease with which they can be used, their long life and the satisfaction of achieving really good results.

As in all gardening operations, the tools that we use must be well-maintained and sensibly handled. Particular care must be taken to keep them sharp and free from rust, and to avoid the risk of overstrain by trying to cut thick hard wood for which they were not designed.

THE PRUNING KNIFE

A good knife is one of the basic tools of the gardener. A number of different shapes of gardening knives are produced, the majority straight-bladed.

A straight-bladed knife has a value in pruning, especially for trimming back damaged tissues or paring smooth the rough surfaces left by a saw or pruner, but its use for pruning is limited unless a fair degree of skill has been achieved. As will be seen from the sketch, a proper pruning knife has a curved blade and handle, the latter being gripped by the whole hand. The thumb is used to hold the stem to be cut firmly in position and to prevent it from sliding away when pressure is exerted. This may seem to be a somewhat risky, not to say painful procedure but, whereas with a straight-bladed knife the blade is passed through the stem, with the pruning knife the blade is drawn across the stem, with a movement of the whole forearm. The curve of the blade is thus brought into play, ensuring a perfectly clean cut, without any squeezing of the hand or alteration of the relative positions of thumb and blade.

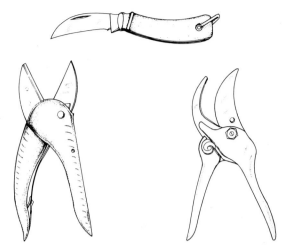

Pruning knife (top) and secateurs (above), showing the anvil-type, left, and scissors-type, right.

SECATEURS

Most people find secateurs the most convenient tool with which to prune, and provided that they are of good quality and properly maintained, excellent results can be achieved. But if they are allowed to become blunt or, worse still, if the blades are twisted or strained by trying to cut stems that are too thick or hard, then it becomes impossible not to bruise the tissues or make rough, jagged cuts. With some designs it is possible to change the blades or replace worn parts, other secateurs have to be returned to the manufacturer for sharpening.

There are two main types of secateur in use today. In the first, a straight-edged, D-shaped cutting blade cuts down on to a bar, or anvil, of softer metal, gripping the branch firmly and making a clean cut. In the second, a convexly curved blade cuts against, but not on to, a fixed bar, which acts as a 'thumb' in holding the stem firmly in position. This type has one advantage in that the cutting blade and bar together come to a much finer point than in the anvil secateur, thus making it easier to manoeuvre between two branches which are growing closely together. A third type is sometimes seen, in which two convexly curved cutting blades cross as in a pair of scissors, the stem being held securely between them.

Whichever type of secateur is used, the stem should be positioned so that it is cut by the base of the blade, where it is firmly held. If the tip is used it is difficult to make a really clean cut and there is a risk of the blades being strained or forced apart.

PRUNING SAWS

The most convenient tool with which to prune larger branches is without doubt a suitable saw. Here again, different types are available, with straight or curved blades, and with the teeth set at various angles.

The English pruning saw has a straight, tapering blade with teeth on both sides, one set to give a fast, coarse cut, the other producing a smoother finish. The taper is useful when working in a limited space, but care must be taken to avoid damaging other branches with the teeth on the back of the blade.

The Grecian saw has a curved blade, tapering to a fine point. The teeth are on one side of the blade only, and are set to be used with a single drawing action. As in the pruning knife, this combines with the pistol-grip handle and the curve of the blade to produce a quick, clean cut, even in a confined space between other branches.

A folding pruning saw, in which the blade closes down into the handle when not in use, is also useful for making large cuts, and can be easily carried without damage to the person or clothing.

SHRUB PRUNERS

Essentially these are a larger version of a pair of secateurs, with blades of similar shape, but with the handles extended to 15 or 18 inches in length (37–45 cm). This gives increased leverage and

Grecian pruning saw (left) and shrub pruner (right).

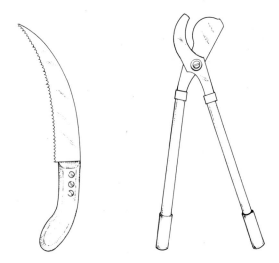

enables even the toughest stems to be cut through, provided that they can be gripped within the jaws of the pruners.

The use of such a tool may be somewhat limited, especially in the smaller garden, but they are of value where a lot of rough, heavy work is involved.

HAND SHEARS

These come within the category of pruning tools, and since hedge-cutting is likely to be a time-consuming job in the garden, it is important to have shears with a good cutting edge, and which are light, well-balanced and comfortable to use, even over a period of several hours.

Powered hedge-trimmers are available which greatly reduce the labour and time involved in this operation.

MAKING THE PRUNING CUT

When considering how to maintain shape and balance in a shrub, we have seen the importance of the growth buds. One of the objects of pruning is to divert the food passing up the stem into one or more of these buds, to produce growth in a particular direction. This is done by always making the cut immediately above a bud and as close to it as possible without damaging it. The cut is started on the opposite side of the stem to the bud, and level with it; it will, of course, be necessary to hold the blade of the knife or secateurs at a slight angle, to avoid damaging or cutting into the bud, but this should be as near to the horizontal as possible, to make a small wound which will heal comparatively quickly. If the angle of the cut is too sharp, not only will the surface area of the wound be much larger, but the food supply available for the bud will be considerably reduced. The drawings overleaf show correct and incorrect positions for the pruning cut.

Every pruning cut must be finished absolutely cleanly with no rough edges, torn or loosened bark, squeezing or bruising of the stem. Any of these will lead to the interruption of the food supply, the eventual death of this part of the plant and consequent risk of infection from air-borne diseases.

When larger cuts are being made on older wood with a diameter of more than $\frac{1}{2}$ to $\frac{3}{4}$ inch (1 to 2 cm), remove the whole of the branch, cutting cleanly back almost to the join with the next largest branch or the main stem. Traditionally cuts were made as near as possible to the branch or main stem which left a slightly oval shaped cut; modern practice is to cut not quite as severely into the stem to be retained and leave a round shaped cut. It is

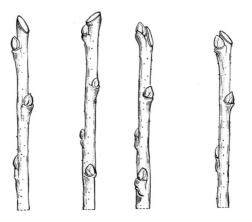

Pruning cuts. The three twigs on the left have been cut too far from or too close to the bud. The twig on the right shows a correct cut.

essential though not to leave a long 'snag' as this will eventually cause die-back providing a source for infection of the main stem. Since a pruning saw or similar tool will be required to cut the larger wood, the rough cut will have to be carefully trimmed with a sharp knife. Again, traditionally, tree wound paints were used to paint over the cut surface to minimise the risk of infection but scientific evidence has since proved that this is not essential – whilst it may well be more aesthetically pleasing to paint the wound, it is not necessary.

A cut made fairly close to the trunk of a tree for removing a large branch.

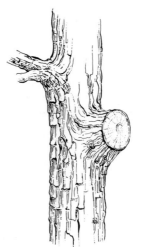

When and how to prune

Although it is possible to define certain broad principles as to the best method and time of year for pruning particular shrubs, it is important to realise the need for treating each plant as an individual within this general framework. It is not unusual to find a group of two or three shrubs of the same sort, or a bed of bush roses, for example, growing in identical conditions and treated exactly alike; the majority thrive, but one plant may be weak and struggling for survival. This may be due to an area of poor soil, root damage or some other purely local condition, but obviously such a plant is going to need different treatment from its more robust neighbours.

It is therefore essential, before starting to prune any shrub, to spend a short time looking at it critically, assessing its state of health, its position and the decorative effect that we are seeking from it. Only by doing this, and bearing in mind what has already been said about growth reaction (see p. 12), can we decide upon the correct method of pruning a particular shrub.

WHEN TO PRUNE

The best time of year to prune a shrub is that which allows it as long a growing period as possible in which to produce wood of the desired type; in general, this means after flowering. Weather conditions can vary considerably from year to year; we must be guided by the stage of growth which the plant has reached and should on no account prune by the calendar.

The time of year recommended for pruning a shrub is not critical – it may extend over a period of two or three weeks, and should the weather be bad on a particular day, the operation can safely be postponed for a short while. Obviously it is not good for either plants or humans to prune during bad weather, especially when the temperature is below freezing, in periods of biting wind, or, when the ground is very wet and liable to compaction by treading among the plants.

HOW TO PRUNE

First, remove any pieces of dead or damaged wood, obviously weak or exhausted branches, and any which may be growing out awkwardly and spoiling the shape of the shrub. Once this is out of the way, we are left with good, healthy material and can see more clearly what may have to be done.

The ornamental shrubs that we grow as specimens in our gardens vary considerably in size, flowering period and other characteristics, but it is nevertheless possible to group them together under certain broad headings as regards their pruning requirements. These groups are based on their habit and on when the decorative growth (i.e. flowering wood) is produced.

DECIDUOUS SHRUBS

This is an important group of ornamental plants, comprising all those shrubs which lose their leaves and remain dormant during the winter. It can be divided into three groups.

Group 1. *Flowering in spring and early summer*

All of these bear their flowers on strong stems produced during the previous growing season, and include forsythia, flowering currants (*Ribes*), *Deutzia*, *Weigela*, *Philadelphus*, and early-flowering spiraeas. Pruning of this group is carried out as soon as possible after the flowers have faded, and consists of the complete removal of all one-year-old stems on which the flowers have been borne. This diverts the energy of the shrub into the young growths, which can already be seen at the base of the older wood, and which continue to develop strongly during the remainder of the summer and autumn, ready for flowering the next year.

It often happens that several young growths develop at the base of a single flowering branch, and it is usually best to cut back to the lowest one, normally the most vigorous, provided that this does not spoil the symmetry or balance of the shrub. This helps to develop a compact, bushy habit, and encourages the production of a regular supply of healthy young growth from low down in the plant, which can be used to replace older, exhausted wood as the need arises.

Group 2. *Flowering in summer and early autumn*

The second group comprises those shrubs which flower in the summer and early autumn, from late July to October, and which bear their flowers at the ends of the current season's growths. One of the best known in this category is *Buddleja davidii*, with long racemes of purple, lilac or white flowers so beloved of butterflies, and, less vigorous in habit, *Caryopteris*, fuchsias and deciduous ceanothus like 'Gloire de Versailles'.

In order to give the flowering wood the maximum time in which to develop, shrubs in this group are pruned as growth starts in early spring. In March or April, when we can see the buds starting to swell, and before the leaves unfold, the previous year's growth, on which the old flower heads can probably still be distinguished, is cut back hard to within one or two buds (or pairs of buds) from the base. At the same time any thin, weak branches and any dead or diseased material, is removed completely.

In this category of shrubs, growth after pruning is often extremely rapid, and it is not unusual for a single stem of a buddleja, cut back to within 12 inches of the ground (30 cm) in March, to have reached a height of 6 or 7 feet (1.8–2.1 m) by the time that it flowers in late July. This raises the problem of wind resistance in exposed situations, and it is the normal practice to minimise this by a light pruning in the autumn, reducing the tallest stems by about a third of their length, and completing the operation at the normal time in early spring.

Buddlejas and ceanothus are good examples of the importance of treating shrubs as individuals, and of knowing something more than just the common name of a plant. A knowledge not only of the botanical family but also of the species to which it belongs may help you to decide which type of pruning it should receive. Thus *Buddleja davidii* and *Ceanothus* 'Gloire de Versailles' both fall within this group, but *Buddleja alternifolia* and the evergreen species of *Ceanothus* like *C. impressus* flower earlier in the year on growths produced during the previous season, and should be pruned immediately after flowering.

A number of small or medium-sized deciduous shrubs grown for the beauty of their flowers (such as *Caryopteris* and *Hypericum*) and evergreens grown for their attractive grey or silver foliage (like *Santolina* or *Helichrysum*) do not need regular pruning to induce them to flower.

They do, however, respond well to cutting hard back just as they are starting to grow in the early spring. As they tend to become straggly and woody with age, early annual pruning encourages the production of new growth from the base, which gives the plant a bushy, well-groomed appearance.

Group 3. Grown for their stems or foliage

Not all deciduous shrubs are grown for the beauty of their flowers. Some, such as the red dogwood (*Cornus alba* 'Sibirica'), some willows, and white-stemmed brambles (*Rubus biflorus* and *R. cockburnianus*) are valued for the decorative colour of their bark in winter. This colour is most conspicuous on vigorous

Prunus triloba flowers more freely if pruned as soon as the blooms fade (see p. 59).

young, unbranched shoots of the current season's growth, and the plants are therefore severely pruned, cutting back almost to ground level, at the end of March or in early April.

Deciduous shrubs with handsome foliage also respond well to similar treatment. The leaves of the variegated dogwoods (*Cornus alba* 'Elegantissima' and 'Spaethii') cut hard back in early spring, or those of *Weigela florida* 'Variegata' pruned immediately after flowering, will be two or three times the size of those on unpruned specimens.

EVERGREEN SHRUBS

In deciding upon the pruning requirements of this prominent group of shrubs, it is worth remembering that we have in this country very few native broad-leaved evergreen shrubs. Most of the evergreens that we grow in our gardens have been introduced from milder climates, and cannot be regarded as being completely hardy during a severe winter.

This has a bearing upon the time of pruning, since cold damage is most likely to occur during the winter and early spring, and can be caused not only by low temperatures and breakage of the branches by snow, but perhaps more often by drying-out and burning of the leaves and young growth after periods of biting wind frost. Such damage is often not immediately noticeable, and after a cold spring, dieback may continue well on into the summer. Evergreens also suffer very badly from periods of hot dry weather, especially if they have recently been transplanted, and much can be done to prevent injury by watering, the application of a generous mulch of straw or garden compost to the soil surface while it is still moist, and by the use of anti-dessicant sprays. Evergreens should have priority for water over deciduous shrubs, which are less likely to suffer in such conditions. When watering, the ground around the roots should be thoroughly soaked, and it is especially beneficial to spray the whole plant in the cool of the evening, which helps to prevent the foliage and young growth from shrivelling.

Evergreens start to make fresh growth much later in the spring than do most deciduous shrubs, and it may well be the end of May or even early June before growth becomes vigorous. This is the best time of year to prune, since then the full effect of the winter can be properly assessed and any damaged growth removed. No evergreen should be pruned late in the summer or autumn as this may stimulate the production of soft new growth, which would almost certainly be damaged by the first sharp frost.

Evergreens growing as specimen shrubs are usually allowed to reach their full size with the minimum of restriction, pruning being confined to the removal of any branches which may develop awkwardly and spoil the natural habit and outline of the shrub. This does not mean that branches, of, say, a camellia should not be cut when in flower for house decoration, even though this is, strictly speaking, pruning at the wrong time of year. In fact if done sensibly and skilfully, it may well be all the attention that the plant will require to maintain its shape and beauty.

Broad-leaved evergreens with variegated leaves are occasionally somewhat unstable, and shoots bearing green foliage may appear anywhere on the plant. These should immediately be cut out, since such reversion, if allowed to remain, can quickly become dominant, when the whole beauty and character of the shrub will be spoilt.

Hedge-cutting

The regular clipping or cutting back to which formal hedges are subjected is as much a form of pruning as that given to specimen shrubs, and the same basic principles apply. The aim is to produce hedges which are thick at the bottom, with the sides well furnished with growth, and tapered so that the width at the top is less than that at the bottom. If this shape can be achieved, the hedge will be less susceptible to damage by snow or high winds, and will form a neat, attractive and practical feature of the garden.

The scented *Osmanthus delavayi* could be used as an informal evergreen hedge (see p. 58).

The choice of plant for a hedge will depend on several factors, whether it is required for ornamental or purely practical purposes, the soil, situation, the height desired, and so on.

Consideration has already been given to the tools required for hedge-cutting, and the availability or otherwise of a power trimmer will also have some bearing on the choice of plant. Laurel and other broad-leaved evergreen hedges should only be pruned with a knife or secateurs, since their leaves will be badly mutilated if shears or a powered machine are used.

AFTER PLANTING

To secure the best results it is very important to make a good start in pruning the hedge, and this varies with the habit of growth. Three groups can be distinguished.

Deciduous

(a) Naturally upright growers are cut hard back after planting, to within 4 to 6 inches of ground level (10–15 cm). Although this entails the initial sacrifice of a certain amount of height, it does encourage vigorous growth during the first season. This growth is again pruned fairly severely in the second year to within 6 inches of the base of this younger wood (15 cm). Examples of hedge plants in this category are thorn, privet, myrobalan plum and snowberry.

(b) Naturally bushy growers for which the initial pruning does not have to be so severe. The leading shoots and the longer side growths are cut back by about one third. Similar treatment in the second year will prevent the hedge from becoming too tall before a good base is established. Beech and hornbeam are two examples of hedges treated in this way.

Evergreen

These are all naturally of a dense bushy habit so that severe pruning in the early stages will only result in the production of a mature hedge which is too wide in proportion to its height. They therefore require no initial restriction, apart from the removal of any untidy straggling growth during the first year, but everything should be done to concentrate growth into the topmost leading shoot. This should, if necessary, be carefully tied up to a cane, until it has reached the desired height of the hedge, which may take several years. Meanwhile, clipping in of the sides of the hedge, coupled with feeding and watering, will not only help the leader to develop, but will assist in keeping the hedge narrow. English yew, perhaps the best hedging plant that we grow, responds well to this treatment, as do all conifers, holly, pyracantha and evergreen cotoneaster.

ESTABLISHED HEDGES

Most plants used for formal hedges need a single clipping once a year, but others, especially privet, quickthorn and the shrubby loniceras, require attention every four to six weeks during the growing season if they are to be kept looking really neat and tidy.

Where only one cut is needed, as with beech or hornbeam, this is usually carried out during late July or August after the initial growth has been made and the stems are beginning to harden and ripen off. Normally this will be sufficient to keep the hedge in order through the winter, but if there is wet weather in August or September, the extra moisture may stimulate further growth, which will require cutting in October.

Coniferous hedges, such as yew and thuja, and broad-leaved evergreens like holly and laurel, also need only one cut, during August or even early September. This must not be done earlier in the summer, since secondary growth will then almost certainly develop, and this will be soft and very susceptible to damage by frosts.

Berrying hedges, pyracantha, cotoneasters and the like, make their growth after flowering and will probably need two cuts. The fully developed young growth is removed when it is beginning to ripen off in late July or August, care being taken to avoid damaging the faded clusters of flowers, which will later bear the fruit. Then in the early autumn, any later growth is carefully cut away, to expose the berries for ripening.

INFORMAL HEDGES

These can be a very attractive feature in a garden, and since they do not receive the regular restrictive pruning given to a formal hedge, involve considerably less maintenance. They do, however, require some attention, for if left completely unpruned they quickly become straggly and lose much of their charm.

The same rules apply as for the pruning of shrubs; for those flowering mainly on the previous year's growth, like deutzias, flowering currant or Berberis × stenophylla, prune immediately after flowering; for those flowering on the current season's growth, such as fuchsias, shrubby potentillas and santolinas, prune in early spring.

Wall shrubs and climbers

The planting space in a garden afforded by the walls of the house or garage, sheds, fences and other supports is often not used to the best advantage. However, these situations provide not only protection if facing south or west, but also a variety of aspects ranging from full sun to complete shade, thus enabling a wide range of plants to be grown.

Nevertheless, great care must be exercised in making the right choice for a particular position. One can imagine the result of planting a vigorous climbing rose, such as 'Albertine' or *Rosa filipes*, capable of reaching a height of 20 feet (6 m) or more, against the low wall of a bungalow or a garden shed, whereas these would be ideal for screening an ugly building or rambling unchecked through the branches of a mature tree. Thorny shrubs should not be planted close to paths, where their habit of catching in the clothing of passers-by becomes a nuisance, and plants which revel in full sun and good drainage will not succeed against north facing walls, a situation where camellias, pyracantha or ivies are quite at home.

We must not forget that, as with open-ground shrubs, a lovely effect can often be achieved by leaving some of the more vigorous climbers virtually unpruned. *Clematis montana*, *Wisteria* or the climbing hydrangea can be encouraged to make their way up into a tree, or allowed to ramble over the roof of a garage or ugly building and, once the growth reaches the light, they will each year produce a beautiful curtain or mass of flower, as well as having a practical, screening effect. *Cotoneaster horizontalis*, the fishbone cotoneaster, on the other hand, will grow quite happily beneath a window, with the occasional removal of a branch growing out from the wall, and will need no tying back or support.

Wall shrubs and climbers can be divided into four groups, according to their habit of growth:
1. Climbers which support themselves by means of aerial roots or sticky tendrils (e.g. ivy and Virginia creeper). These will grow against a flat surface.
2. Climbers with stems, tendrils or leaf-stalks which curl or twine (e.g. wisteria, vines and clematis). These require some artificial means of support.
3. Climbers with hooked thorns or long, scrambling stems (climbing or rambler roses).

31

4. Wall shrubs, which naturally grow as free-standing specimen shrubs, but which in our climate benefit from the protection afforded by being trained against a wall or fence, or which have additional ornamental value when grown in this way.

Most of the above groups require the provision of some form of artificial support against which the plants can be trained. This must be strong enough to support the weight of the mature shrub, which, if one is planting, say, a wisteria, may well be quite considerable. The supports, whether of wire, trellis or plastic mesh, should always be fixed *before* planting takes place; once growth has started it is difficult to fix anything to the wall without damaging the tender young shoots.

A point to be remembered when dealing with vigorous climbers is that branches should be kept well clear of any gutters or drainpipes. The annual growth can easily be disentangled and removed, but with age the main stems of a wisteria, for example, can be 6 inches (15 cm) or more in diameter, and can easily force a down-pipe or gutter away from the wall if allowed to grow behind it.

PRUNING METHODS

The same basic principles apply as for open ground shrubs, but there are two distinct stages: the establishment of a basic framework of branches on which the shrub can develop in later years; regular annual pruning to obtain the maximum decorative effect and to keep the plant under control.

Climbers in group 1, e.g. ivy and *Hydrangea petiolaris*, do not require artificial support, but usually need some trimming of the shoots; this is generally done in late winter or early spring. There is no need to train a basic framework for this type.

Climbers in group 2, such as vines, wisteria and clematis, need support and training to keep them under control. With wisteria or a vine the basic framework is built up in the first couple of years, followed by spur pruning of established plants.

Those clematis which flower in summer, e.g. *C.* × *jackmanii*, do not have a permanent framework as they are cut back hard in February. *Clematis montana* and honeysuckles have a simple basic framework and are pruned when necessary to thin out the flowering shoots.

Some degree of control of shrubs grown against walls is usually necessary if the plant is not to encroach over a path or shade other plants. Not all need wire supports, but it is easier to train the plants against the wall if new shoots can be tied into position.

There are various types of formal training, initially developed

Above: *Lavatera olbia* 'Rosea' is best cut back hard in April (see p. 56).
Below left: *Cistus* can only be pruned when young (see p. 50).
Below right: the Spanish broom should be pruned in March each year,
but do not cut back into the old wood (see p. 62).

for fruit trees but adaptable for use with flowering shrubs. By such training shoots and branches are spaced out to make as uniform a cover over the wall as possible, so that each shoot gets maximum light and warmth for ripening the wood. Training for ornamental shrubs need not be so disciplined as for fruit trees, but it is useful to have a rough outline of a fan or espalier for training in the early stages, which will later give a firm framework for an established bush (see below).

The choice between fan training and an espalier will depend on local conditions, such as the height of the wall and the plant concerned. Fans are generally more suitable for shrubs on lower walls, and espaliers for those that tend to have a strong main stem against a higher wall. Cherries, camellias, Japanese quince, pyracantha and ceanothus are among the plants which will adapt to this formal type of training. Others such as *Garrya elliptica* can be tied in as convenient without forming an initial framework.

Fan training

In the first year cut back the main shoot to about 2 feet (60 cm) from ground level. Allow two shoots to grow out below this cut, one to the left and one to the right. Tie these shoots to bamboo canes at an angle of 45° to the main trunk. In the second winter cut these shoots back to about $1\frac{1}{2}$ feet (45 cm); two more shoots are allowed to grow out in the next summer, and trained one above the first shoot and one from below. These four shoots are each cut back by a third in the next winter.

In subsequent years continue training and tying in the shoots, and prune according to the species (see following pages). It is important to guide the young shoots into their space as they are formed and while still pliable. Any shoots growing away from the wall or otherwise awkwardly placed are removed. Annual pruning of established shrubs will keep the plant looking neat.

Espaliers

Other shrubs are suitable for training as espaliers, pyracantha being a good example. Cut the young plant back to three good buds at about 18 inches to 2 feet (45–60 cm), with the two lower buds pointing in opposite directions. Tie the shoot from the top bud to a vertical support, and train the shoots from the other two buds along canes fixed at an angle of about 45° to the main stem. At the end of the growing season lower the two side branches to the horizontal wires and tie them in. Cut back the vertical leader to a bud about 18 inches (45 cm) above the lower arm, leaving two

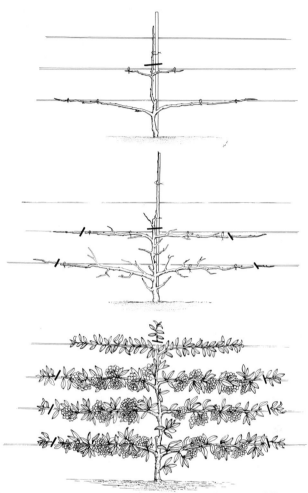

Espalier-training a shrub. Second year, top; third year, middle; established, bottom.

good buds to form the next horizontal arms. Cut back any surplus laterals on the main stem to three buds and prune back the lower horizontal arms by one-third, cutting to downward-facing buds. Repeat this process each year in the autumn until the shrub has filled the required space, and prune back the new terminal growths of the vertical and horizontal arms each summer, to keep the tree at its required size.

PRUNING ESTABLISHED CLIMBERS

The time taken to build up the basic framework of a climber varies according to the situation and vigour of the particular shrub, and the method of training used, but once the available space has been evenly covered, regular annual pruning can begin.

The method and the time of pruning depend upon the principles already described (pp. 23–27), being generally carried out either immediately after flowering, or else just as the growth buds are beginning to swell in the early spring. However, plants growing against a warm wall will often be two to three weeks ahead of those growing in the open ground and growth will sometimes continue late into the autumn or even early winter in sheltered positions. For this reason it is wise to check plants in early autumn and tie back any young unflowered wood as this is naturally brittle and may be damaged in the autumn gales.

On old climbers and wall shrubs it may well happen that one of the main framework branches becomes damaged or exhausted, and stops flowering or producing any vigorous young growth. Before starting regular annual pruning, it is advisable to look for weakness of this sort and if any is found, the whole stem should be cut back to healthy wood, tying in a strong young branch to fill the space left in the framework.

A number of climbers, particularly the climbing sorts of roses and some clematis, have the habit of producing young growth mainly in the top half of the plant, leaving the lower part of the main stems bare of leaves and flowers. With such a plant, the remedy is to cut back severely one or two of the main stems to within $1\frac{1}{2}$ to 2 feet (45–60 cm) from the ground in early spring, at the same time feeding and watering generously. Such drastic treatment will usually induce the dormant buds on the old stems to start into growth so producing vigorous young wood from low down in the plant. By treating a proportion of the main stems in this way each year, it is generally possible to rejuvenate it quite quickly.

Bareness of this sort at the base of a climber could usually have been prevented by correct treatment in the first year after planting. Fairly severe initial pruning, cutting the main stems back to about 18 inches (45 cm) from the ground will not only reduce the strain on the root system before it is properly established, but will increase the number and vigour of the young basal growths which will form the framework of the plant.

(See also the Wisley Handbook, *Climbing and Wall Plants*.)

Examples of the different *Clematis* groups (see pp. 50–51): *C. montana* (above), pruned immediately after flowering; *C. orientalis* (below left), pruned as growth starts early in the year; and *C. × jackmanii* (below right), pruned hard in early spring.

Roses

The diversity of habit of growth in roses necessarily entails a variety of pruning techniques, nevertheless, all roses are deciduous flowering shrubs, and the principles and methods of pruning already outlined apply to them just as much as to a forsythia or a buddleja. However, they can be divided into two broad groups:

1. The true species and their hybrids; the old garden roses (Damasks, Bourbons, Gallicas, etc); the hybrid musks and the so-called shrub roses.

2. The modern display roses, bush or standard hybrid teas and floribundas (large- and cluster-flowered), climbers, ramblers, polyanthus and miniature roses.

AS SPECIMEN SHRUBS

Where space permits, strong-growing roses like R. *filipes*, R. *longicuspis* and some of the more vigorous ramblers and climbers can be encouraged to grow up into trees or over a building, and allowed to ramble freely without any pruning restriction other than the occasional removal of any dead or damaged wood. They will quickly provide a curtain of flower each summer and usually retain their vigour for many years with the minimum of attention.

Shrub roses grown as specimen bushes do benefit from a certain amount of regular pruning, the method and time of year of this operation depending upon their habit of growth. The treatment is that recommended for deciduous flowering shrubs (pp. 24–25); those producing their best flowers on the previous year's wood are pruned immediately after flowering, the remainder just as growth is starting in early spring. It is important to allow sufficient room when planting this type of rose, since many of them are capable of developing into large shrubs and any restriction will only spoil their naturally graceful habit.

PRUNING NEWLY PLANTED ROSES

Most shrub roses will not require any attention for the first twelve months until they have become properly established, but the display roses all benefit from quite severe pruning in the early spring immediately following planting.

Bush roses planted during the first half of the dormant season (up to about mid-January), will need no further attention until the early spring. Late-planted roses can either be pruned at the time of planting, or left until the developing buds indicate that root growth is beginning. In both cases the treatment is severe, bush and standard hybrid teas having any weak growths removed completely, and the remainder cut back to within two or three buds of the base; floribundas, with their greater vigour, can be left at three to five buds. Such hard pruning not only reduces the demands made on the root system of the plant before it has become properly established in its new position, but encourages the production of strong growth from the base which will eventually form the open-centred, evenly shaped plant that we desire.

Newly-planted ramblers and climbers should also be pruned quite severely, the stronger stems to within 12 or 18 inches (30–45 cm) of ground level, the weaker being cut back to 3 or 4 inches (7–10 cm), to encourage vigorous growth. It is especially important to do this with climbers since most of them do not naturally produce new wood from the base of the plant, and must be encouraged by initial pruning to build up a good framework from the start.

PRUNING DISPLAY ROSES

Cluster- and large-flowered roses

These all flower on the current season's growth, and benefit from quite severe annual pruning, not only to improve the quality of the flowers, but also to keep the plants bushy, and to maintain a constant supply of vigorous young wood.

Early March to early April is usually the time favoured, especially in cold districts, but many rose growers now prune when the plants are completely dormant (December–January). The advantage with early pruning is that one is less busy in the garden at that time, and it is perfectly alright for sheltered gardens in towns or cities, where the temperatures in cold weather can be as much as 10°F (5°C) higher than in open country. If, however, there is any risk of the plants being subjected to severe frost after pruning, then it is best to delay this until the developing buds at the top of the stems show that growth is just beginning. In open situations, where the plants are exposed to strong winds, it is advisable to remove about a third of the top growth from tall bushes in the early autumn, to minimise wind resistance and consequent 'rocking' of the plant.

A small point worth noting is that cluster-flowered roses, with

Above: *Chaenomeles*, the Japanese quinces, should be spur pruned like apples after flowering (see p. 50).
Below: *Sambucus* are kept in shape with regular cutting back each spring (see p. 62).

Salix daphnoides, one of the most valuable willows for winter effect when cut back hard annually in late winter (see p. 61).

their greater vigour, usually start into growth 10 to 14 days before large-flowered roses, and therefore need to be pruned first. For the same reason the large-flowered roses are pruned more severely than cluster-flowered roses, in order to encourage a more vigorous growth reaction. First remove all damaged wood and thin, weak branches on the large-flowered roses. The strongest (the thickest) of those remaining are shortened back to four or six buds, the less vigorous to two to four buds from the base of the shoot. Cluster-flowered roses are pruned to six or eight buds on the stronger stems and four to six on the weaker.

Rambler roses

True ramblers have only one period of flower, in June and July, and should be pruned as soon as the flowers have faded, although, if this is for any reason impossible, they can be dealt with in early spring, but with less satisfactory results.

The long whippy stems which have borne the flowers on short side growths, are cut right down to ground level, and the developing young growths which are easily distinguished as they are smooth and unbranched, tied in to take their place. It is on these growths that the next year's flowers will be borne. These will now receive all the nourishment of the plant, and will continue to grow, until by the end of the season they may be 10 or 12 feet (3-3.6 m) long. If there should not be enough of these new stems to provide adequate cover on the support, a few of the older growths may be retained for a further year, the laterals (the side shoots which have already flowered) being pruned back to two or three buds.

Weeping roses are pruned in the same way as ramblers, the lax young growths usually being trained out over a wire frame.

Climbing roses

Climbers have arisen in various ways. Some are sports from existing large-flowered or cluster-flowered cultivars, others are of more complex parentage as the result of deliberate crosses, while the recent appearance of medium-growing pillar cultivars is evidence of the plant breeder's success in developing a very free-flowering and not too vigorous group well suited to the more limited space available in present-day gardens.

In contrast to the ramblers, climbing roses flower on current season's growth and rarely produce fresh growth from the base, and hence it is necessary to train out a framework of permanent branches which remain on the plant for a number of years. From these short laterals, flowering growths are produced, which are pruned each year in late February or March to within two or three buds from their base. Weak and dead wood is, of course, removed first, and any old or exhausted main branches are cut out and replaced by young, unflowered wood.

It sometimes happens that a climbing rose will make a lot of vigorous growth, and if this is tied in vertically against its support, only the buds at the top of the branches will develop lateral shoots, and consequently there will be few flowers. By training these strong growths out horizontally, or even slightly below the horizontal, the flow of the sap will be checked, the buds further down the stem will produce laterals, and the amount of flower will be greatly increased.

Heathers

The varieties and forms of heaths and heathers, *Calluna, Erica, Daboecia* and the like, which go to make up this extremely decorative group of evergreen shrubs, provide a gay and colourful display of flowers and foliage during every month of the year. Although many of them are native to Britain and might therefore be expected to be well suited to our climate, in the artificial conditions of garden cultivation, some pruning is beneficial in keeping the plants healthy and well shaped, and in improving the length and quality of the flower spike. With some types of heathers, the life of the plant can be extended from about seven years to fifteen years before requiring replacement if clipped (pruned) annually.

They may be divided into three groups:
1. Those that flower in summer, from June to October.
2. Those that flower in winter, from November to April.
3. The tall-growing tree heaths.

SUMMER-FLOWERING

Such pruning as this group requires is best carried out in early to mid-March, and amounts to no more than a very light trimming, the previous year's flower heads being cut back to a point just below the bottom flowers of the spike. Heathers are unlikely to produce shoots from old wood so this will be quite sufficient to keep that plants bushy, and prevent them from straggling and losing their shape.

In the first few years, while the plants can still be treated as individuals, a pair of secateurs is the best tool to use for trimming but once they have grown together and cover the ground, a pair of shears will be quicker and more convenient. But vary the angle at which the blades of the shears are held, since this produces a more natural effect than the flat 'hedge-trimmed' effect sometimes seen.

Not all the summer-flowering heathers need to be pruned every year. Cultivars like *Calluna vulgaris* 'Foxii Nana' or 'J.H. Hamilton', and *Erica vagans* 'Valerie Proudley' have a naturally low, compact habit, and can be allowed to grow without any restriction, retaining their beauty for many years.

The effective life in the garden of many of the taller, summer-

Above: *Rubus* 'Tridel', pruned annually in June or July (see p. 61). Below: a privet hedge will need trimming several times in the summer (see p. 29).

Above: *Santolina*, cotton lavender, shaped to a rounded hummock (see p. 62).
Below: *Piptanthus* should be pruned in late winter (se p. 59).

flowering heathers is limited and after some seven to nine years, despite regular trimming, they begin to deteriorate. The flower spikes shorten, and growth becomes hard and woody; once this stage is reached, it is better to take some cuttings and raise a new stock of young plants, or to replace the old group with a different cultivar.

Many heathers have brightly coloured foliage which is effective throughout the whole year, often changing in winter to deeper tones of orange and flame. Plants of this type may be left until the end of March or early April before being trimmed.

WINTER-FLOWERING

Erica herbacea (carnea), *E.* × *darleyensis* and their numerous cultivars can be relied upon to flower from early November to March, and are thus the mainstay of the winter garden. They are all low-growing, rarely exceeding 2 feet in height (60 cm) and mostly have a compact and bushy habit, so that the need for pruning is greatly reduced. Pruning every second or third year will suffice for many, while others can be left alone.

Erica herbacea 'Springwood White' is a good example of a variety which, although very low-growing, spreads extremely rapidly and can easily grow into and smother its less vigorous neighbours. To keep it within bounds pruning is confined to trimming back the sides of the group.

All winter-flowering heaths should be pruned immediately they have finished flowering, since they start to make growth almost at once, and if pruning is delayed for too long, the next season's display will be reduced.

TREE HEATHS

The taller-growing species, like *Erica lusitanica*, *E. terminalis* and the beautiful but rather tender *E. australis*, need no regular pruning beyond the occasional removal of an old, exhausted branch, or one which is growing out awkwardly and spoiling the shape and outline of the plant.

Heavy snow may break down the stems of *Erica arborea*, or they may be split by severe frost, while the soft tip growths of *E. australis* and *E. erigena (mediterranea)* are often affected by cold, causing them to die back later. Any such winter damage should be removed in late April or May, when the risk of severe weather is over, and fresh growth will quickly cover up the scars.

(See also the Wisley Handbook, *Heaths and Heathers*.)

A guide to the pruning of some popular shrubs and wall plants

Abelia. Medium-sized shrubs which need a sheltered position in cold districts. Little attention needed, apart from the removal of any winter-damaged shoots in March, at the same time cutting out any long growths which may spoil the shape of the shrub.

Abutilon. For a warm wall or mild climate. Remove any damaged wood at the end of the winter, and maintain a good, even shape.

Acer. Most species develop into trees, but many of the Japanese maples are grown in shrubby form. Beyond occasional removal of an awkwardly placed branch, they require no pruning.

Actinidia. Vigorous climbers, which need a strong support and regular pruning to keep them under control. Prune in winter, no later than mid-January, as the sap starts to rise early, cutting back the previous year's growth to one or two buds. In late July or August reduce the new shoots to 6 to 9 inches (15–22 cm), and if further growth occurs, this should be treated in the same way a month or so later.

Akebia. Strong-growing twining plants, which are best allowed to ramble freely over a wall or into a tree, when little pruning will be needed, other than the removal of any dead or damaged wood at the end of the winter.

Aloysia. The lemon-scented verbena, *Aloysia triphylla*, is a delightfully aromatic shrub for a sheltered corner near a path, where the leaves are within easy reach of passers-by. It is liable to be damaged in a severe winter, and can be pruned just as growth is beginning in the spring.

Amelanchier. No regular pruning needed, but thin out weak and crowded growth as soon as flowering has finished in May.

Ampelopsis. Similar treatment to *Vitis* (p. 64).

Aronia. Suckering shrubs noted for their autumn colour. Cut out old branches in late winter if necessary.

Artemisia. Prune the previous year's growth hard as growth starts in early spring, sacrificing flower to maintain a bushy, shapely plant with attractive grey foliage.

Arundinaria. See Bamboos (p. 48).

Aucuba. No regular pruning needed. Keep in shape, and remove any dieback or dead wood as it occurs.

Azalea. See Rhododendron (p. 60).

Passiflora caerulea, a rampant climber unless controlled; the side growths should be cut back in February (see p. 58).

Azara. If grown against a wall, prune at the end of May or early June to keep in shape. Specimens in the open require no regular pruning.

Bamboos. No regular pruning needed, other than the removal of any dead canes at the end of the winter. Cut these off right down at ground level; the old stumps are not easily seen, and can cut the hand like a razor.

Bay. See *Laurus nobilis* (p. 56).

Berberidopsis. A beautiful, slow-growing, evergreen climber for a shady, sheltered position. No regular pruning needed.

Berberis. No regular annual pruning is required, but keep the centre of the plant open by cutting out old stems to ground level, or back to young vigorous growth. Deciduous berberis are pruned in the late winter, after the beauty of the fruit is over; evergreen types are pruned in April, or after flowering in May or early June.

Broom. See *Cytisus* (p. 52).

Buddleja. Three types are commonly found in gardens:

Buddleja alternifolia, flowering in early June along growth made in the previous year. Immediately after flowering cut out branches which have borne the flowers.

Buddleja davidii and its forms, flowering in July and August on the current year's growth. Prune hard in early spring, just as growth starts.

Buddleja globosa, flowering in June on the tips of growth made during the previous year. No pruning needed, apart from cutting out any weak or damaged wood in March, and maintaining the shape.

Bupleurum. As a mature shrub, it may become sprawling and untidy; it will then respond to moderately severe pruning in early spring.

Buxus (box). Box hedges, topiary and box edging will need clipping at least twice during the summer to keep them neat and tidy. An old hedge can be renovated by cutting it hard back at the end of April or in early May. When grown as a specimen shrub, box requires no regular pruning.

Caesalpinia. Any long growths from the previous year are cut hard back at the end of February.

Callicarpa. Thin out any crowded growth in early February, retaining as much as possible of the younger wood.

Calluna. See heathers (pp. 43–46).

Calycanthus. When necessary, thin the bushes in late winter, retaining as much of the young wood as possible.

Camellia. Require no regular pruning. Any awkward branches such as those growing out from the wall should be removed. This can be done in late April, just as growth is beginning or at flowering time, when the cut branches can be used for indoor decoration.

The many cultivars of *Camellia japonica* have a somewhat stiff habit of growth, but the hybrid *C. × williamsii*, and in mild districts *C. reticulata*, can be trained out against the wall, which provides extra protection for the early flowers. Apart from this training, no regular pruning is required.

Campsis (*Bignonia* and *Tecoma*). Prune the growths made during the previous summer back to within two or three buds from the old wood in February or early March.

Caragana. No regular pruning, but after flowering shorten any long growths on young plants, to encourage them to form shapely bushes.

Caryopteris. Cut back the flowering shoots of the previous year in February or early March. Strong growths will need to be shortened to 2 to 4 inches (5–10 cm) each year and thin ones either shortened to within a bud or two of their base or removed altogether.

Ceanothus. The evergreen and deciduous types need quite different training:

1. The spring-flowering *evergreen* ceanothus are usually grown against a wall, and bear their flowers on short growths produced in the previous year. They are pruned each year immediately after flowering, to within 4 inches of the base (10 cm) of flowered shoots. The short side growths are pruned back almost to the

framework branches; this can be done with secateurs or, if there is plenty of growth, the plant can be clipped over with shears.

2. The *deciduous* group of late summer- and autumn-flowering ceanothus, of which 'Gloire de Versailles' is perhaps the best known, flower on the current season's growth, and are therefore pruned each year in February or March. Remove any thin, weak wood, and shorten the strong shoots back to two or three buds from the base.

Celastrus. Vigorous twining shrubs, with attractive fruits in autumn. They are difficult to confine within a limited space, and are seen at their best when allowed to scramble up into a tree. In these conditions, no regular pruning is needed.

Ceratostigma. In early March, cut back the old flowering shoots to firm, well-ripened wood. In many areas these shoots are cut by frost to ground level.

Chaenomeles. When grown as bushes the Japanese quinces need regular annual pruning to prevent them from developing into a tangled mass of growth, with the flowers hidden in the centre of the plant. After flowering shorten the side growths back to two or three buds, to encourage the formation of spur growth similar to apples, to which these plants are related. They make excellent fan-trained wall shrubs, the regular pruning needed to keep them within bounds resulting in the production of short flowering growth along the main framework branches.

Chimonanthus (wintersweet). When growing against a wall or fence shorten the secondary shoots to within one or two buds of the base as soon as the flowers have faded in early spring. Bushes in the open only require thinning when the growth becomes too crowded.

Choisya. No regular pruning. Old sprawling bushes with bare stems may be cut back fairly severely into the old wood during May to improve their shape.

Cistus. Mediterranean evergreen shrubs, apt to suffer during a cold winter. Prune at the end of May, removing any damaged growth and if necessary pinching out the tips of the shoots to keep them bushy. In later years very little pruning is possible, as they resent being cut back into the hard old wood. It is best to replace old shrubs with vigorous young plants.

Clematis. For pruning, clematis may be divided into four groups:

1. Species flowering in early summer on the previous year's growth (e.g. *C. montana*, *C. chrysocoma*). Prune immediately after flowering, cutting back almost to the base of the shoots which have borne the flowers.

2. Species flowering in late summer and autumn on the current year's growth (e.g. *C. orientalis*, *C. tangutica*, *C. rehderiana*).

Prune just as the buds are beginning to swell in early February, cutting back severely, almost into the old wood, or leave unpruned if there is sufficient room.

3. The Florida, Lanuginosa and Patens groups of large-flowered hybrids which flower on the previous years's growth, are only lightly pruned after flowering, since they occasionally produce some later flowers on the young growth.

4. The Jackmannii, Texensis and Viticella groups of large-flowered hybrids which flower on the current season's growth, are pruned severely in February or early March, often cutting back nearly to ground level.

The parentage of some of these garden hybrids is complex, and it is not always easy to distinguish the group to which a possibly unnamed plant belongs. In such cases a safe method of pruning is to examine the plant in early February, and look for any pairs of fat buds which are just bursting into growth. By cutting back to the uppermost of such buds, whether they are at the top of the plant or nearly at ground level, the desired effect will be achieved, and one will not be sacrificing potential flowering wood. (See also the Wisley Handbook, *Clematis*.)

Clerodendrum. *C. trichotomum* and its variety *fargesii* make tall shrubs which require no regular pruning, apart from the removal of some sucker growth if they become too invasive. *C. bungei*, if not killed to the ground by frost, should have the stems cut back to firm, healthy wood in April.

Clethra. No regular pruning needed, but spreading sucker growth must be kept under control.

Colutea. Shallow-rooting, leguminous shrubs which benefit from being cut hard back in the first spring after planting to encourage the development of a firm root system. Adult bushes need little pruning.

Convolvulus. *C. cneorum*, a very beautiful low-growing, silver-leaved shrub, needs no pruning if planted in a sheltered position at the foot of a warm wall. An occasional long shoot may have to be shortened back during May.

Cornus. The tall-growing flowering dogwoods, *Cornus florida* and *C. kousa*, are specimen shrubs which need no regular pruning. The bushy types like *Cornus alba* and *C. stolonifera*, with coloured bark grown for winter effect, or with variegated leaves, are pruned severely at the end of March, to encourage vigorous growth.

Coronilla. No regular pruning needed.

Corylopsis. No pruning required.

Corylus. Prune back the vigorous growths of the purple-leaved and golden-leaved nuts in February or early March each year, to induce plenty of strong new shoots, as these bear the best coloured leaves.

Cotinus. *C. coggygria* (*Rhus cotinus*), Venetian sumach or smoke tree, is usually allowed to develop naturally into a large specimen bush, with the minimum of restriction. The purple-leaved forms can be pruned hard each year in late March, as with *Cornus alba* or *Corylus*, to produce longer shoots with large leaves.

Cotoneaster. Most members of this diverse family require no regular pruning when they are grown as specimen shrubs, beyond the maintenance of a pleasing shape and outline. When used for hedging they must, of course, receive regular clipping appropriate to their particular evergreen or deciduous quality.

Cytisus (broom). The popular hybrid brooms, 'Dorothy Walpole' and the like, must be regularly pruned in order to keep them well shaped. Immediately the flowers have faded, the young growth is shortened by about two-thirds of its length, taking care not to cut too far back into two-year-old wood. Old plants seldom break satisfactorily when cut into old hard wood, and are best replaced with a young plant.

Cytisus battandieri, the Moroccan broom, has a much freer habit, and very ornamental flowers and foliage; it makes an excellent large specimen shrub for a lawn or border, but is perhaps seen to best advantage when trained against a sunny wall. Pruning then consists in tying back the young growth after it is fully developed, during August, at the same time thinning out by removing a few of the oldest main stems.

Daboecia. See heathers (pp. 43–46).

Daphne. The daphnes are mostly low-growing compact shrubs which need no regular pruning. The garland flower, *Daphne cneorum*, sometimes tends to straggle, and can be carefully cut back to shape it after it has flowered in April and May.

Deutzia. All kinds flower on growth made during the previous year, and are pruned as soon as the flowers have faded, cutting back to strong developing young shoots. The periodic removal of one or two stems down to ground level will stimulate the production of vigorous basal growth.

Diervilla. Not to be confused with *Weigela*, diervillas have a somewhat suckering habit of growth, and need little pruning other than the removal in March of a few of the older stems, and a thinning of any excess material.

Dipelta. Treat as for *Weigela* (p. 64).

Eccremocarpus. Cut back to firm stems of the previous year's growth in February. If cut to the ground in a severe winter remove the dead stems in order that the new growth may develop unhindered.

Elaeagnus. All make large specimens if allowed unrestricted growth. The deciduous types respond well to hard pruning in the early part of the year, particularly the grey-leaved E. *angustifolia*, while the variegated forms of E. *pungens* comprise some of the finest of our evergreen shrubs, requiring the minimum of control. The latter have, however, a tendency to reversion, and any green-leaved shoots which may appear should be cut out as soon as they are noticed.

Embothrium. No regular pruning required. After a hard winter some damaged growth may have to be removed and, occasionally, careful shaping after flowering will be beneficial.

Enkianthus. The only pruning needed is to prevent the plants becoming straggly and losing their shape and balance.

Erica. See heathers (pp. 43–46).

Escallonia. When grown in the open, no annual pruning is necessary, although the occasional removal of a few of the long, arching growths immediately after flowering, will help to keep the plant in shape. When grown as a hedge, or trained against a wall, escallonias are pruned or clipped as soon as the flowers have faded.

Eucalyptus. If left alone, eucalyptus naturally develop into very large trees, but they can successfully be kept within bounds by 'stooling', or cutting the stems hard back, to within 12 to 18 inches of ground level (30–45 cm). This is done annually in March or April, after the risk of severe frost is past. The plant makes very rapid growth, and wind resistance can be a problem, but this system of pruning greatly improves the anchorage of the root system.

Eucryphia. Both the evergreen and deciduous types naturally form rather erect, shapely specimens, and need little or no pruning, other than the removal of dead or damaged wood.

Euonymus. The deciduous species need no regular pruning, but the evergreen E. *fortunei* var. *radicans* and E. *japonicus*, often used as a seaside hedge, will need clipping or shaping at least once a year.

Exochorda. Tall-growing shrubs which, if allowed plenty of room in which to develop, need little pruning. Overgrown specimens usually respond well to cutting back hard in early spring.

Fabiana. A beautiful low shrub for a sheltered position, needing little restriction, although long growth can be shortened back after flowering, in May or June, to encourage bushiness.

Fatsia. With such bold and handsome foliage, the maintenance of shape and balance is important, but otherwise no regular attention is needed.

Forsythia. Annual pruning immediately after flowering in early

53

spring is necessary, especially for *F. suspensa* when grown against a wall or fence, for which its lax habit makes it particularly suitable. *Forsythia × intermedia* 'Spectabilis' and other strong-growing types have a very vigorous growth reaction to severe pruning, and flower production may suffer in consequence, although they make good hedges, flowering freely if clipped to shape once or twice during the growing season.

Fothergilla. No regular pruning needed.

Fuchsia. A number of cultivars and hybrids can be regarded as reasonably hardy. The old stems are usually killed to ground level during the winter, and these should be removed as soon as the young growth appears in April or May.

Garrya. When grown as a specimen shrub this fine winter-flowering evergreen requires no more pruning than is needed to maintain a good even shape. If trained against a wall, shorten the previous year's growth back almost to the framework branches after flowering.

Gaultheria. No regular pruning is needed. *Gaultheria shallon* sometimes forms a dense, matted thicket which needs to be cut back hard to bring it under control. This is best done towards the end of April.

Genista. The tall-growing species, like the brooms, do not respond well to cutting back into old wood, but if lightly trimmed at intervals during the summer, even as young plants, they will usually retain a good, bushy habit. *Genista hispanica*, the Spanish gorse, and *G. lydia* need no regular treatment, indeed, careless pruning could easily destroy their naturally attractive habit of growth, but any dead branches should be removed immediately.

Gorse, see *Ulex* (p. 63).

Griselinia. This popular evergreen shrub for mild and maritime districts requires no regular pruning, but it is often necessary to shorten some of the longer growths, to keep the bush shapely and within limits. This is best done between April and the end of June.

Halesia. Cutting out of the oldest flowering shoots and shortening any long growths is sometimes worthwhile immediately after flowering, in order to keep a shapely and attractive specimen.

Halimium. Low-growing, slightly tender relations of *Cistus*, requiring similar pruning.

Hamamelis. Only prune when necessary to shorten very long shoots which tend to destroy the symmetry of the bushes. March is the best time, but the unwanted flowering branches can safely be cut for indoor decoration.

Hebe. Attractive low-growing evergreen shrubs, some of them slightly tender. No regular pruning is needed, apart from the removal of any winter damaged shoots in May, but most of them will readily produce fresh growth when treated in this way.

Hedera (ivy). On walls or fences close clipping with shears is usual in May or June. Later in the summer the plants will need further attention, any long young growths being removed with the knife or secateurs. Odd straggling growths on tree ivies should be removed in early May.

Hedysarum. Shorten the flowering growth of the previous year back almost to its base in late February; retain the best of the young stems, and cut out completely any thin, weak wood.

Helianthemum. To keep these plants neat and bushy, prune after flowering at the end of July; they can be clipped with shears or secateurs, and will soon make fresh growth to flower the next year.

Helichrysum. Low-growing, often aromatic shrubs, many with grey leaves, they all respond to fairly severe pruning at the expense of the flower, the previous year's growth being cut back almost to its base in March or April.

Hibiscus. The cultivars of H. syriacus have a tall, erect habit, and can be left almost unpruned. If desired, they can be cut back just as growth is beginning in early May, to form close, shapely specimens.

Hippophaë (sea buckthorn). Little pruning is necessary.

Honeysuckle. See Lonicera (p. 57).

Hydrangea. The well-known Hydrangea × macrophylla (hortensis) carries its flowers on the tips of one-year-old stems which arise from the base of the plant. No regular pruning is needed, although, when an old branch ceases to flower properly, cut it out to ground level, to keep the shrub well thinned. Leave the dead flower heads on the plant throughout the winter, since they afford a measure of protection to the terminal buds, but as soon as the new leaves begin to unfold in the spring and it is possible to see the extent of any frost damage, trim the plants back to sound growth.

Hydrangea paniculata produces its flowers on the current season's growth, and is therefore pruned annually in late February or early March, cutting back to within one or two pairs of buds from the base of the previous year's growth.

The climbing hydrangea, H. petiolaris (H. anomala ssp. petiolaris) is a vigorous self-clinging plant capable of reaching the top of a high wall or up into a large tree. Little attention is required, but if it grows out too far from its support, it may be necessary to cut back some of the stems in the early spring.

Hypericum. The low-growing Hypericum calycinum and H. × moserianum flower freely in summer and autumn when cut down to within a few inches of the ground at the end of March each year. The taller, shrubby types can be treated in much the same way, or they can be only lightly trimmed to remove any winter damaged shoots, and allowed to develop naturally to form rounded, medium-sized free-flowering specimens.

Ilex (holly). Hollies growing as individual specimen shrubs should be lightly trimmed each year in the late spring, just as they are beginning to make new growth. Neglected or badly shaped plants may be dealt with at the same time, and usually respond well to quite severe cutting back into old wood. Holly hedges may be clipped with shears in early August.

Indigofera. Responds to hard pruning in March, cutting back the old wood almost to ground level, from where the new shoots will quickly develop, to flower in the summer and autumn.

Ivy . See *Hedera* (p. 55).

Jasminum. Winter jasmine, *J. nudiflorum*, and *J. mesnyi* (*primulinum*) in mild localities, give the best results when the flowering shoots are cut back fairly hard each year as soon as the blooms fade. With *J. officinale* thin the long growths in late summer after flowering, or in February or March.

Kalmia. No regular pruning required.

Kerria. As soon as the flowers have faded cut out as much as possible of the old wood, either back to where young growth is appearing, or else down to ground level. The variegated form sometimes produces a green shoot, and this should be removed at once.

Kolkwitzia. Prune after flowering in July, cutting back to new young growth, which will maintain the attractive arching habit.

Laurel, common. See *Prunus laurocerasus* (p. 60).

Laurel, Portugal. See *Prunus lusitanica* (p. 60).

Laurus. *L. nobilis*, sweet bay or bay laurel, is often grown as a formal clipped bush or tub plant, and careful shaping with secateurs is needed, two or three times during the summer. If allowed to grow freely, no regular pruning is necessary.

Lavandula (lavender). Cut off the old flower stalks and lightly trim the bushes as soon as the colour of the flowers has faded. Old plants, especially of old English lavender, tend to become open and straggly with age, and can be cut hard back in late April; they do not always respond to this severe pruning, and for a hedge a compact type such as 'Hidcote' should be chosen.

Lavatera. *L. olbia* 'Rosea' is a slightly tender but strong-growing shrubby mallow, which is best pruned back quite severely in April.

Leptospermum. No regular pruning other than the removal of any damaged or straggling growths.

Leucothoë. Very little pruning is needed. Thin out a few branches from time to time at ground level, but do not shorten them back, as this will spoil the attractive, arching habit of the plant.

Leycesteria. Thin out old and weak shoots and remove any winter damage or die-back as growth starts in spring. Plants can also be stooled, or cut back to ground level each year, to get the full winter effect of the bright green bark.

Ligustrum (privet). Privet hedges require clipping several times during the summer if they are to be kept really neat and tidy, and the vigorous root system exhausts the soil in its immediate vicinity, making it difficult to grow other plants nearby. Some species, such as *Ligustrum japonicum* and *L. lucidum*, are very handsome specimen evergreens and, when allowed to develop naturally, require no regular pruning.

Lilac. See *Syringa* (p. 63).

Lithospermum. As an old plant it tends to sprawl and become matted and untidy. Careful pruning after flowering will help to keep it within bounds.

Lonicera (honeysuckle). Most of the climbing honeysuckles are best pruned after flowering, cutting away some of the old weak growths, and either tying back the developing young shoots or, perhaps more effectively, allowing these to hang down over their support. *Lonicera japonica* 'Halliana' and 'Aueoreticulata' with gold-netted leaves, are nearly evergreen, with a different habit of growth, flowering on the young wood of the current year; if it is necessary to keep them under control, they can be pruned in the spring.

The shrubby honeysuckles benefit from an occasional shortening of long growths, which may be spoiling the shape of the plant, and this can be done after flowering in the summer, but apart from this no regular pruning is needed. *Lonicera nitida*, like privet, requires frequent clipping when grown as a hedge, if a really neat appearance is to be maintained.

Lupinus arboreus (tree lupin). Cut out any thin and weak wood in February or early March, and shorten back the strong growths of the previous year almost to their base.

Lycium. An occasional thinning of surplus growth in summer after flowering is beneficial. Bushes that have outgrown their position may be cut hard back in March.

Magnolia. The deciduous magnolias make magnificent specimen shrubs when allowed to develop to their natural size with the minimum of restriction. Any pruning that may be needed, especially if they are trained against a wall, is done immediately after flowering. *Magnolia grandiflora*, the summer-flowering evergreen species, requires a different approach. It is usually given the protection of a warm wall and the pruning and training necessary to keep it within bounds is carried out as growth is beginning in May.

Mahonia. No regular pruning is required, but the plants occasionally show a tendency to produce one or two long bare stems, which spoil their shape. These are shortened well back in late April or May. *Mahonia aquifolium*, the Oregon grape, makes an attractive low hedge, and should be carefully shaped with the knife or secateurs at the same time of year.

Menziesia. Little regular pruning, apart from some thinning and cutting out of weak growth where necessary.

Myrtus. The common myrtle, *M. communis*, needs no regular pruning. In colder parts of the country it may suffer during a severe winter, and damaged wood will need to be removed when the weather warms up in the spring.

Neillia. Flowers in early summer on growth made during the previous year. Prune after flowering.

Olearia. Most of the evergreen daisy bushes are somewhat tender, but grow very well near the sea. No regular pruning is needed.

Osmanthus. Evergreen shrubs which need only occasional attention to keep them in good shape. New growth develops freely after pruning in May or early June.

Paeonia. The shrubby tree peonies fall within the scope of this work, and the hardier species, such as *P. delavayi* and *P. lutea*, need little regular attention beyond occasionally thinning out a few of the older stems down to ground level. The many beautiful forms of the moutan peony, *P. suffruticosa*, are winter hardy but start to grow so early in the year, that the soft young shoots are frequently damaged by frost, even where some temporary protection has been given. By the end of May the risk of severe cold is usually over, and the damage can be repaired by cutting back to healthy wood.

Parthenocissus. See *Vitis* (p. 64).

Passiflora. The passion flower, *P. caerulea*, can become a rampant grower in the right situation, and needs to be kept under control. Restrict to a few main branches by cutting back the side growths to within two or three buds of the old wood in February each year and the young shoots on which the flowers are borne will quickly form a curtain down over the plant.

Periwinkle. See *Vinca* (p. 64).

Pernettya. No regular pruning. Shorten back any long straggly growths after flowering to keep the plants bushy; if covered with berries they can be cut and used as decoration in the winter.

Perovskia (Afghan sage). Grey-leaved aromatic shrubs for a well-drained sunny position. Prune in early March almost to the base of the previous year's growth.

Philadelphus. All types flower on one-year-old wood, and are pruned immediately, after flowering in summer. Cut back to the strongest of the young shoots, which will already be developing lower down in the plant. Any weak growths should be pruned severely, to encourage the production of vigorous shoots from the base of the plant.

Phillyrea. Prune as *Osmanthus* (p. 58).

Phlomis. No regular pruning is needed, but cut back any straggly growth in late April or May, to keep the plant bushy.

Photinia. No regular pruning; shorten long straggling shoots of the deciduous species in early winter, and of the evergreens in May, just as growth is beginning.

Phygelius. May be cut down to the ground in a severe winter, and damaged stems are cut off when new growth starts. If they remain undamaged the stems are pruned back to healthy wood in March or April.

Pieris. No regular pruning needed, but some may occasionally be needed to keep the plant evenly shaped and balanced.

Piptanthus. Remove old worn-out wood and shorten long young shoots by about two-thirds of their length in late February. On walls spur prune back to the main framework branches.

Pittosporum. No regular pruning. Cut out any winter damage during May.

Polygonum. Rampant, twining climbers, which are most effective when allowed to grow freely, without any pruning. If it has to be kept to a limited space, pruning should be done during the late winter, while the plant is still dormant.

Poncirus. Only requires enough pruning to maintain an even shape. Makes an excellent, quite impenetrable hedge; clip back in early June.

Potentilla. First-class shrubs for a limited space, with a naturally bushy habit and a very long flowering period. No regular pruning is necessary apart from cutting out a few of the oldest stems down to ground level in early March.

Privet. See *Ligustrum* (p. 57).

Prunus. Most of the ornamental plums, cherries and peaches do not respond well to pruning, and are best left alone. If some wood has to be removed, the safest time to do this is while the plants are still in flower, or immediately afterwards, to minimise the risk of disease. There are two low-growing *Prunus* species, however, which are exceptions to this rule, *P. glandulosa* and *P. triloba*. These flower very freely if the young branches are cut back to within two or three buds of the old wood as soon as the flowers are over, in April or early May each year.

Prune both the common (*Prunus laurocerasus*) and Portugal (*Prunus lusitanica*) laurels with a knife or secateurs rather than clipping with shears (to avoid cutting the leaves) although this does, of course, take much longer to do. The best time for such trimming is late May or early June, but when grown as a formal hedge, the work is done six to eight weeks later. Where it becomes necessary to cut bushes or hedges back into hard wood to rejuvenate them, late April or early May is the best time.

Pyracantha. When grown in the open these evergreens need only occasional pruning to keep them within bounds. They make excellent hedges, which usually need clipping twice a year, first soon after flowering, care being taken to avoid damaging the immature fruits, and again in late August or early September. By then some secondary growth will have appeared, and this must be removed to expose the ripening berries to the sunlight. Similar treatment is given to pyracanthas trained against a wall or fence.

Rhamnus. Prune and thin occasionally; the evergreen species in April or May, deciduous types during the winter.

Rhaphiolepis. Little pruning is required other than that necessary to keep the plant in shape.

Rhododendron. Generally no regular annual pruning is necessary. Young growth of the evergreen types can be pinched back from time to time, to keep them within bounds, and the same applies to the deciduous azaleas. Dead-heading immediately after flowering, by preventing the plants from wasting their energy in setting seed, has a marked effect upon the following year's display, and should be done whenever possible. When it is necessary to prune large straggling bushes with bare stems, cut them hard back to the old wood in late winter or early spring. This may mean the loss of one or two seasons' flower, but most types respond well to such treatment, and quickly produce vigorous new growth. In general species and hybrids with smooth, peeling bark, such as *R. barbatum* and *R. thomsonii*, resent such severe pruning, and fail to develop satisfactorily.

Rhodotypos. A medium-sized shrub with a similar habit of growth to Kerria, and responding to the same method of pruning (see page 56).

Rhus. Most species need very little pruning, but the stag's horn sumach, *R. typhina* and its variety 'Laciniata', which are grown for foliage effect and autumn colour, can be cut hard back each year in April, to within one or two buds of the old wood. Do not prune earlier, as die-back often follows pruning when the plants are dormant. See also *Cotinus*.

Ribes. Prune *Ribes sanguineum* after flowering, in April, removing a few of the older branches to allow light and air to ripen the wood properly, and at the same time keeping the plant evenly balanced. The flowering currants make attractive hedges, and are treated in the same way as forsythia, clipping the young growth to shape once or twice during the growing season.

Robinia. A few species are shrubby in habit, notably *R. hispida*, the rose acacia, which is best grown in a sheltered position or trained against a wall, as the wood is very brittle and easily damaged by wind. *Robinia pseudoacacia* 'Frisia', although naturally tree-like in habit, responds well to stooling, cutting the one-year-old stems hard back almost to their base in March, to produce the maximum effect from the attractive, pale golden leaves.

Romneya (Californian tree poppy). The old growth normally dies back to ground level in the winter, and should be left until the new shoots appear in the spring before being cut off.

Rosa. Where they have room to develop, the species and many of the larger shrub roses make effective individual specimens. Many of them benefit from regular annual pruning, the methods varying according to their particular habit of growth. Fuller details will be found on p. 38–41. For details of pruning climbing and rambling roses, see pp. 41–42.

Rosmarinus (rosemary). Overgrown or straggly bushes can be cut back to shape into the old wood in April. Light pruning of the tips of the growth at the end of May will help to maintain a good habit, and hedges should be trimmed or clipped at the same time of year, after flowering.

Rubus. Prune the white-stemmed blackberries for winter effect, cutting the old stems down to ground level at the end of March every year in order to encourage vigorous growth.

Shrubby species such as *R. deliciosus* or its fine hybrid 'Tridel' flower on the previous year's wood, and are pruned annually in June or July, after the flowers have faded.

Ruscus. No regular pruning required, but any dead or damaged growth is cut out at the end of the winter.

Ruta. Best pruned annually in April or early May, cutting back the one-year-old wood almost to its base, sacrificing flower in order to produce a neat hummock of blue-green foliage.

Salix (willow). Like the forms of *Cornus alba*, some willows with highly coloured bark are very valuable for winter effect, especially if they can be grouped near water. Pruning is done annually at the end of March or early April, cutting the young growths hard back to within a bud or two of the old wood. *Salix alba* 'Vitellina' and 'Chrysostella', and *S. daphnoides* are three of the best sorts to treat in this way.

Salvia. The common sage, *S. officinalis*, and its coloured-leaved forms, are attractive, low-growing shrubs for the edge of a path or paving. Older plants often become straggly, but respond well to cutting back the bare stems in the spring. There are a few Mexican species which are worth trying in a warm, well-drained and sheltered situation, such as *S. microphylla* (syn. *S. grahamii*) and its variety *neurepia*; these are also pruned in the spring, just as growth is beginning, when the full extent of any winter damage can be properly assessed.

Sambucus. Prune and thin the bushes in early March to keep them shapely and attractive. When grown for coloured foliage as is the golden-leaved variety *S. nigra* 'Aurea', cut hard back to within a bud or two of the old wood in March.

Santolina. Like rue, cotton lavender is best pruned each year in April or early May, cutting back almost to the old wood, and sacrificing flower in order to produce a rounded hummock, of silver-grey foliage. It also makes an excellent dwarf hedge.

Sarcococca. Low, suckering shrubs which need no regular pruning.

Schizophragma. Fine self-clinging climbers, similar in habit to *Hydrangea petiolaris*, but even more spectacular in flower. They require similar pruning.

Senecio. Apart from occasional shaping in the spring if an old plant begins to sprawl or needs keeping within bounds, no regular pruning is required.

Skimmia. A naturally low-growing shrub with a rounded outline. Needs no regular pruning, and any shaping that may be necessary should be done in the late spring.

Solanum. If space permits, *Solanum crispum* is very effective when allowed to ramble freely over a low support. To keep it trained against a wall, pruning is done in the early spring, just as growth is beginning, any thin weak stems being removed, and the healthy vigorous shoots tied in to take their place.

Sorbaria. Formerly included under *Spiraea*, these vigorous shrubs flower in July and August on the current season's growth. Prune in February or early March, cutting back to within two or three buds of the old wood.

Spartium. The Spanish broom. Prune each year in March, even as a young plant, to form a bushy foundation, reducing the young growth by about half its length, and taking care not to cut down into very old, hard wood.

Spiraea. Most benefit from regular pruning, but it is important to distinguish between the two main groups. Those like *S. arguta* and *S. prunifolia* which flower in the spring or early summer on growth made during the previous year, are pruned immediately after flowering, cutting back to where strong young shoots can already be seen further down the stem.

The second group comprises the late summer flowering types, such as *S. japonica* or *S. douglasii*, which flower on the ends of the the growths produced during the current season; these are pruned in early spring, cutting back to within two or three buds of the older wood.

Stachyurus. Pruning is seldom required. Shorten any long growths in April after flowering to keep the bushes shapely.

Staphylea. No regular pruning, except as necessary to maintain shape and balance. After flowering remove any old branches on which there is no healthy growth.

Stephanandra. Cut out old growths to ground level after flowering, or in winter, to encourage production of vigorous shoots from the base.

Stewartia (Stuartia). No regular pruning required.

Stranvaesia. Occasional thinning of crowded growth and the maintenance of the shape and balance of the shrub, is the only attention required.

Styrax. Tall shrubs or small trees with an attractive outline, which must be preserved by careful training and shaping when young. Mature plants need no regular pruning.

Symphoricarpus. Most of the snowberries have a dense, suckering habit of growth, and such pruning as is necessary is aimed at keeping the plants within bounds, and thinning out some of the old, weak stems each year in the late winter.

Syringa (lilac). Remove the flower heads as soon as they have faded, and thin out any weak growth in the centre of the plant. Lilacs vary considerably in their vigour, and those of a tall, erect habit will need a more restrictive form of pruning to keep them within bounds, the one- or two-year-old stems are reduced by at least half or two-thirds of their length, immediately after flowering. Old, exhausted specimens which have outgrown their position in the garden, can often be successfully rejuvenated by really severe pruning; details are given on pp. 13–16.

Tamarix. The spring-flowering types are pruned immediately after flowering. Those which flower in late summer and autumn on the current season's growth (e.g. *T. pentandra*) are pruned back in February or early March to within two or three buds of the old growth.

Teucrium. When grown against a wall or fence, shorten back the side growths to within one or two buds of the main branches in March. Otherwise no pruning is necessary.

Trachelospermum. No regular pruning needed.

Ulex (gorse). The double-flowered form, which is usually grown in gardens, requires no regular pruning, but old leggy bushes can be given a new lease of life by sacrificing a season's flower and cutting the stems down to within a foot or so of the ground in early April.

Vaccinium. Little pruning required, other than the maintenance of shape and balance and the removal of dead or damaged wood.

Verbena. Similar treatment as for *Aloysia* (see p. 47).

Viburnum. Both the deciduous and evergreen species should be allowed to develop to their natural size without any regular pruning. Very dense, crowded growth may be thinned during the winter, but care must be taken not to spoil the characteristic outline of the shrub as, for instance, the horizontally tiered branching of *Viburnum plicatum* var. *tomentosum*. Laurustinus, *V. tinus*, can be grown as a hedge, and is trimmed during May, together with the other evergreen types.

Vinca (periwinkle). Established groups which have grown together to form a dense ground cover, can be clipped over with shears in early spring, but this should not be necessary every year.

Vitis, Ampelopsis and **Parthenocissus**. These three plants are often confused, the main distinction between them lying in their method of support – *Ampelopsis* and *Vitis* climb by means of coiling tendrils, whereas *Parthenocissus*, which includes the so-called Virginia creeper (correctly Boston ivy), has tendrils which are flattened at the end and actually cling to the surface.

All the ornamental vines are strong-growing plants and are most effective when allowed to grow without restriction. If they have to be confined within a limited area, pruning must be carried out when the plants are completely dormant, preferably in December or no later than the middle of January. The sap starts to rise very early, and there is a risk of severe bleeding from the open cuts if pruning is delayed until February.

Weigela. The growth made during the previous year is cut back as soon as the flowers have faded. By then the developing young shoots should be clearly visible further down the stem, and it is on these that the following year's display will be borne.

Wisteria. Regular pruning twice a year not only increases the amount of flower, but also enables even a vigorous mature plant to be kept within a fairly confined space, under reasonable control. The young growth develops into thin, trailing shoots, eventually as much as 10 to 12 feet long (3–4.8 m), which are cut back in early August to within about 6 inches of the main stems (15 cm). In December or January, the short spurs formed by this summer pruning are shortened further back, to where the plump flower buds can easily be distinguished from the smaller, flattened growth buds.